MEDITATION
ILLUMINATED (

Peace !

Jay Rians

MEDITATION ILLUMINATED

*Simple Ways to Manage
Your Busy Mind*

JOY RAINS

Whole Earth Press • BETHESDA, MD

Whole Earth Press
A Division of Key Seminars, Inc.
P.O. Box 34816
Bethesda, MD 20817

Publisher's Cataloging-in-Publication Data
Rains, Joy.
Meditation illuminated : simple ways to manage your
busy mind / Joy Rains.
p. cm.
ISBN 978-0-9886699-0-1
Includes bibliographical references.
1. Meditation. 2. Meditation — Handbooks, manuals, etc.
3. Relaxation. 4. Stress (Psychology) — Prevention. I. Title.
BL627 .R3265 2013
158.1/2 — dc23
2012954614

Printed in the United States of America

Design by Kachergis Book Design
Editing by Barbara E. Kahl
Author photo by Sukhwant K. Shimkaveg Photography

For those with busy minds,

may you find moments of peace

☙ CONTENTS

✍ PREFACE

I've grappled with anxieties for as long as I remember.

When I was six years old, my father nicknamed me "Miss What If" because of my incessant questions. *What if I can't swim back to shore? What if we get stuck on the top of the roller coaster? What if Fluffy runs away?* Worry was my constant companion.

In my late 20s came a deep yearning for peace of mind. Intrigued with the idea of meditation as a path to peace, I devoured a myriad of meditation books, articles, workshops, events, and retreats. But an understanding of the essence of meditation still eluded me, as if the practice was veiled in mystery. I'd find small pieces of the puzzle but could not see the whole picture clearly.

So I started exploring meditation piece by piece until a coherent picture emerged. I discovered that meditation was not about stopping thoughts, but about becoming aware of them. I learned how to watch these thoughts and allow them to pass. I learned how to focus on my breath and steady my mind. I became less reactive. Less judgmental. Less stressed. More grounded. More accepting. More relaxed.

After decades on this journey, I now bring others the simple explanations I longed for years earlier. My hope is to offer you ideas and practices that can transform your life—and help you find clarity, inspiration, and peace on your path.

MEDITATION
ILLUMINATED

✍ INTRODUCTION

Welcome!

This is a "how to" guide—a primer for those wanting to learn how to meditate. Within these pages, you'll find new material and material synthesized from different teachers and traditions. I consider this style of meditation to be *restorative meditation* since it can help restore the mind to a balanced state.

Part I focuses on the nature of the mind and the "STUFF" it churns out. Part II illuminates the essence of meditation—what the practice is and how it works. Part III describes exactly how to meditate. Part IV focuses on applying the skills to daily life. Part V offers details on preparing for practice, strategies for approaching "obstacles" to meditation, and instructions for 21 varied meditation practices. The Appendix contains a brief overview of the science behind the benefits of meditation, and the Glossary contains a handful of key terms.

If you'd like to jump right into practicing meditation (Part V), you can familiarize yourself with the language and concepts used by reading the summary page at the end of each chapter leading up to Part V.

Here's a sampling of some of the language used in the book, along with a couple of key points to remember:

- ✒ The word "practice" is used to refer to the actual discipline of meditation (*he has a daily meditation practice*), to refer to a specific exercise in meditation (*here's a practice that focuses on the breath*), or to refer to the actual doing of meditation (*practice daily for the best results*). If you don't remember anything else, just remember this: practice, practice, practice.

- ✒ The words "inhale" and "exhale" are used to describe either an action (*inhale as you count one, and exhale as you count one*) or to describe a focal point for your attention (*notice the length of your inhale and the length of your exhale*). Taking a moment to focus on your breath can help focus your mind—and you can do this anywhere, anytime.

The following pages contain instructions and recommendations that can be adapted to fit your needs. Meditation can be practiced in a wide variety of ways, so I wish you the freedom to discover the ways that are right for you.

PART I

**STORIES, THOUGHTS,
URGES, FRUSTRATIONS,
AND FEELINGS**

1 ✐ THE NATURE OF THE MIND

Developing awareness of the content of your mind

Meditation is a discipline of training the mind through the practice of awareness

To understand the practice of meditation, let's start with an understanding of the nature of the mind.

Just as it is the nature of the heart to beat, it is the nature of the mind to generate content. I call this content STUFF, an acronym for:

Stories
Thoughts
Urges
Frustrations
Feelings

STUFF is an important part of functioning in the world —it helps people navigate their way in life. Meditation is not a practice of suppressing your STUFF. It is a practice of becoming aware of your STUFF, so you can see it clearly and directly. By practicing awareness while you are meditating, you are training your mind to become more aware in daily life as well. This direct awareness can help you to *respond consciously* to life's events, rather than to *react unconsciously.*

Let's take a closer look at what all the letters of the acronym STUFF represent.

Stories

People make sense of their worlds by creating stories based on their experiences, biases, and dispositions. This behavior stems from an ancient survival mechanism—for example, when our ancestors anticipated that food would be scarce in winter, they could stockpile provisions.

People create stories all the time—stories about themselves, about others, and about events in their lives. Although creating stories can serve as a survival mechanism to help prepare for the future, sometimes the stories serve no positive purpose and simply create stress.

Consider the young professional who misses his train and is late for his job interview. He thinks, *I'm late. They're going to think I'm irresponsible. I won't get the job.*

I'm never going to find work. While it's true the young man is late, the rest is conjecture. He's creating stories that are, in turn, creating stress.

People often create stories to fill in gaps of unknown information and interpret the events in their lives. Yet these stories can also produce unintended effects, such as stress and misinterpretation.

Consider the following example: Paula approaches Liz and thinks, *Why is Liz scowling at me? I bet she's still angry that I borrowed her shoes without asking.* Liz is actually thinking, *I wish I hadn't eaten that greasy food for lunch. My stomach is in knots. I feel so sick.*

Some stories are true and useful, other stories are simply illusions. As the old saying goes, "Don't believe everything you think."

Thoughts

It is widely believed that the average person generates anywhere from 50,000 to 70,000 thoughts per day. The mind is constantly generating thoughts, from thoughts about big issues (*How can we create more peace in the world?*) to thoughts about small issues (*Should I wear the blue scarf or the green one?*) to judgments of liking or not liking (*I love this weather!*) to worries about the future and regrets about the past (*Why didn't I speak my mind?*).

Thoughts often happen at lightning-fast speed, with

the same thoughts cycling through the mind repeatedly, or with the mind darting from one thought to a totally unrelated thought.

If you could listen to someone's darting thoughts, you might hear: *Ugh! I wish I could be in a different department than Denny. He is so distracting with his constant chatter. He reminds me of my old boyfriend. I wonder what Tim is up to these days. Last I heard he was in San Francisco. I love that city! Maybe I can go there for summer vacation, if I can afford a vacation this year, that is. Better start saving and cut back on those trips to Starbucks. I want to cut back on caffeine, anyway. I was up half the night last night and felt so jittery...*

The rampant activity of the mind has been compared to that of a restless monkey that becomes drunk and then is bitten by a scorpion.[1]

Urges

Strong desires and impulses create urges. Some people struggle with urges for food, others with urges for drugs, or gambling, or surfing the Internet, or shopping, or any multitude of desires.

If you could listen to someone's food cravings, you might hear: *I could really go for a big piece of cheese—that tangy taste in my mouth and that soft texture like it's melting. With a salty, crunchy cracker. And some sweet, juicy grapes to set it off. Sweet, salty, and savory. Ah, I can almost taste it. Cheese! Yum!*

Urges can burst into the mind uninvited and take up a lot of mental real estate, especially when addictions are involved.

Frustrations

Frustrations can kick in when urges aren't satisfied, or when life doesn't unfold according to plan.

If you could listen to the thoughts of someone who is frustrated in a crowded parking garage, you might hear: *I don't want to wait in this line of cars! This is going to take forever. I can't believe this bottleneck. And now I'm trapped. I'm never coming here on a weekend again!*

Frustrations can stem from the negative judgments and meanings people give to the events of their lives.

Feelings

Experiencing feelings is a vital part of life. Yet often people can be consumed with feelings about past events and imagined future events.

Sometimes people engage in internal running narratives that can amplify and intensify their feelings. Someone with regrets about a misstatement might be thinking: *I can't believe I said that. I shouldn't just blurt out the first thing that comes out of my mouth. Grrrr! I'm such an idiot. Stupid! Now he's never going to want anything to do with me again. Next time I see him, he's probably going to pretend he doesn't even know me.*

Consider Mark Twain's famous comment about feelings of anxiety: "I am an old man and have known a great many troubles, but most of them never happened."

Chapter 1 Summary

- ☙ *Meditation trains the mind through the practice of awareness.*

- ☙ *The mind generates content called* STUFF *(Stories, Thoughts, Urges, Frustrations, Feelings).*

- ☙ STUFF *is an important part of functioning in the world—it helps people navigate their way in life.*

- ☙ *Meditation is not a practice of suppressing your* STUFF. *It is a practice of becoming aware of your* STUFF *so you can see it clearly and directly. This direct awareness can help you respond consciously to life's events, rather than react unconsciously.*

Coming next: Learn about the attributes of STUFF in Chapter 2.

2 ✎ THE NATURE OF STUFF

Understanding the nature of STUFF

Let's take a look at the main attributes of STUFF.

STUFF *is subjective*

Although STUFF may seem like objective reality, it is actually subjective and filled with judgments. Consider this story about two shoe salesmen:

When the salesmen arrive on a remote island, they realize all the natives are barefoot. One salesman contacts the home office and says, "Bad news! No opportunities for sales. No one wears shoes." The second salesman reports back to the home office, "Great news! No one wears shoes! Many opportunities for sales!"

People's judgments and interpretations become their realities. Consider the following situation where one person interprets an experience as fun, while another interprets the same experience as dangerous: A family with a young child travels home from Disney World on an extremely turbulent airplane. As the plane pitches, the little one giggles with delight. He loves it; the bouncing plane is like another Disney ride. When the plane finally stabilizes, the woman in the next row sighs with relief, releases her white-knuckled grip on the armrests, and exclaims, "Thank goodness that's over!"

As William Shakespeare wrote in *Hamlet*, "There is nothing either good or bad, but thinking makes it so."[2]

STUFF *is habitual*

Thousands of years ago our ancestors developed negative, habitual thought patterns as survival mechanisms. Vigilant thoughts helped protect them from becoming the tiger's lunch.

Although developing negative thought patterns may have served our ancestors, this sort of thinking does not always serve well in modern times. Many people find negative thoughts—for example, thoughts that are angry, compulsive, or anxious—frequently arising. These negative thought patterns can help people navigate their way in life, but often, they can be the root cause of stress.

In the article "Everything That Can Go Wrong Listed," the satirical newspaper, *The Onion,* spoofed negative thinking, writing that "a worldwide consortium of scientists, mathematicians, and philosophers is nearing the completion of the ambitious, decade-long project of cataloging everything that can go wrong . . . the list is widely believed to include hundreds of trillions of potential scenarios." Here's an excerpt from page 55,623:

> *run in stocking . . . phone system down . . . glass eye falls out during speech . . . hairdresser quits . . . lose $60 at bus stop . . . meat goes bad . . . computer crashes during lengthy download . . . grain elevator explodes . . . gored by moose . . . sour cream runs out . . . mother-in-law hates you . . . ignored by waiter . . . $2 winning scratch-off washed with pants . . . humidity makes hair frizzy . . . neck breaks while clowning around . . . everyone finds out you're a fraud . . . strike out with bases loaded . . . earth gets thrown off axis . . . pen dries out in middle of class . . . bite violently down on inside of cheek while eating sloppy joe . . . mother throws out beloved old stuffed hippo . . . wrong backing-vocals tape played . . .* [3]

Although many people habitually engage in negative thinking, it does not always serve well. Meditation can cause a shift in habitual thinking. Please refer to the Appendix for scientific information on how meditation can actually change patterns of the brain.

STUFF *is impermanent*

STUFF may seem permanent, but it changes. Each moment is new. Each breath brings a new beginning and a new ending. Feelings change, thoughts change, and situations change. Your STUFF is not solid and permanent, although it may feel that way. Consider the following old story:

> Centuries ago, a farmer began his early morning chores only to discover that his prize horse had run away through a broken fence. A neighbor later said to him, "It's too bad that your prize horse ran away." The farmer replied, "Too bad? How do I know that the loss of the horse is a bad experience?"
>
> Several days later, the prize horse returned—but not alone. With him were nearly a dozen of the finest wild horses that roamed the plains. Seeing the return of the prize horse together with the other horses, the neighbor came over and said to the farmer, "What good fortune you have experienced!" The farmer again replied, "Good fortune? How do I know that having all these horses is good fortune?"
>
> The farmer's young adult son, obviously pleased with the new horses, selected one for his own. On his first attempt to ride bareback, however, the horse bucked violently, throwing the young man off and

breaking his leg. Learning of the situation, the neighbor came over and said to the farmer, "What a terrible experience to have happened to your son." The farmer replied, "Terrible experience? How do I know that the breaking of my son's leg is a terrible experience?"

A week later, a vicious warlord came storming through the countryside, conscripting every able-bodied young man to fight in his bloody battles. The farmer's son was passed over. And so it goes.[4]

No event exists in isolation; rather, a continuum of events forms the fabric of one's life. Yet an "inner judge" seemingly rules on each situation as if it is separate from the whole. When the gavel bangs with a verdict of *bad!*, disappointment sets in. When the gavel bangs with a verdict of *good!*, happiness arises—until the event changes, which it inevitably will.

Chapter 2 Summary

    ↬ STUFF *is subjective.*

    ↬ STUFF *is habitual.*

    ↬ STUFF *is impermanent.*

Coming next in Part II: Learn about the essence of meditation and how meditation works, starting with how STUFF relates to meditation in Chapter 3.

PART II

MEDITATION
ILLUMINATED

3 ⌒ THE ESSENCE OF MEDITATION

Interrupting your STUFF *by adding neutral content*

Interrupt your STUFF *and slow it down*

Imagine that the "prizes" on a wheel of chance are comprised of your STUFF. The wheel spins so quickly that the individual descriptions are illegible, blurring as they whiz by. These blurred descriptions represent the cycling STUFF in the mind. Just as inserting a flapper will slow the wheel of chance, introducing a "flapper" in meditation will interrupt and slow the cycle of STUFF. The "flapper" in meditation is called an "anchor."

Shift your attention to your anchor

In meditation you interrupt your cycle of STUFF by introducing an anchor, which is an *object of awareness* that does not distract you with its meaning. One of the most common anchors is the breath. You shift your attention from subjective content (STUFF) to neutral content (the anchor, e.g., the breath). This attention shift interrupts and slows your STUFF—and also helps train your mind to focus.

The attention shift is repeated continually throughout practice

You shift your attention to your anchor repeatedly throughout your practice time, sometimes as often as every few seconds. Just as the repetitive motion of doing abdominal crunches can build your core strength, the repetitive refocusing on your anchor can build your power of awareness.

For example, let's say a busy executive has a big project due. If you could listen in to her thoughts, you might hear: *I don't know how I'm going to meet my deadline—I have so much to get done between now and then. I don't even know if Sam will have time to gather the data I need. I don't know how I'll get this done in time. I feel so overwhelmed!*

But now, let's say this executive is meditating while these thoughts are cycling through her mind. She is using her breath as her anchor, bringing her awareness back to her breath each time her mind wanders. This time her experience may be different: *I don't know how I'm going to meet my deadline.* (Now she notices that she is inhaling, and she notices that she is exhaling.) *I have so much to get done between now and then. I don't even know if Sam will have time to gather the data I need.* (She is once again aware of her breathing.) *I don't know how I'll get this done in time.* (She notices the length of her inhale and the length of her exhale.) *I feel so overwhelmed.*

As she becomes more experienced in focusing on her anchor (her breath), her time meditating may be more like this: *I don't know how I'm going to meet my deadline.* (She notices that she is inhaling, and she notices that she is exhaling. For the next few breaths, she notices her lungs filling with air as she inhales and emptying as she exhales.) *I have so much to get done between now and then.* (Now she notices that the air is cool when she inhales and warm when she exhales. For the next few breaths she is able to keep her complete attention on her breath.) *I don't even know if Sam will have time to gather the data I need.* (She is once again aware that she is breathing. She notices the pace of her next few breaths, paying attention to where her inhale begins and ends and where her exhale begins and ends.) *I don't know how I'll get this done in time.* (She notices the length of her inhale and the length of her exhale and finds she can keep her complete attention on the next few breaths.)

As she becomes even more experienced, she may find that the length of time she can remain completely focused on her anchor becomes longer.

Whether she remains focused on her anchor for one second, for one minute, or for a longer period of time, she is interrupting her STUFF with awareness of her breath—her anchor. With the repeated shift of awareness to her breath, she is training her mind to focus.

She is also adding space to her STUFF—by adding neutral content with the awareness of her anchor. It's like she is shifting the mechanism of her mind out of "drive" and letting it rest in "neutral."

Chapter 3 Summary

- ✑ *An anchor is an object of awareness that should not distract you with its meaning.*

- ✑ *One of the most common anchors is the breath.*

- ✑ *Shifting your attention to your anchor interrupts and slows your* STUFF—*and trains your mind to focus.*

- ✑ *This attention shift is repeated continually during practice, sometimes as often as every few seconds.*

- ✑ *Awareness of your anchor adds space to your* STUFF *and helps your mind rest in "neutral."*

Coming next in Chapter 4: Learn how adding space to your STUFF loosens your attachment to it and helps you see it clearly.

4 ⇝ HOW MEDITATION WORKS

Stepping back and witnessing your STUFF

Loosening attachment to your STUFF

Try this: Place your hands in front of you. Join your two index fingers together so they're touching and form one unit. Let's say your left finger represents *life,* and your right finger represents your *response to life.* Now separate your fingers so there's space between them. That's what meditation does—it adds space between life and your response to life—by training your mind to pause amidst your STUFF.

This space can help you loosen your attachment to your STUFF. For example, if a friendly dog is vying for your attention and you don't respond, he may walk away. For that particular moment, the attachment between you and the dog has loosened. The same principle works with your STUFF. Continually shifting your attention from your STUFF to your anchor will loosen the attachment between you and your STUFF.

Twentieth century spiritual teacher Eknath Easwaran illustrates this point by comparing thoughts to actors.

Life is a kind of play in which we are called upon to play our part with skill. But in meditation we are sometimes more like the audience, while our thoughts are the actors. If we could go backstage, we could see all the actor-thoughts getting made up. Anger is there putting on his long fangs. Fear is rattling his chains. Jealousy is admiring herself in the mirror and smearing on green mascara. Now, these thought-actors are like actors and actresses everywhere: they thrive on a responsive audience. When Jealousy comes out on stage and we sit forward on our seats, she really puts on a show. But on the other hand, what happens if nobody comes to see the performance? No actor likes to play to an empty house. If they're real professionals, they might give their best for a couple of nights, but after that they're bound to get a little slack. Jealousy doesn't bother with her makeup any more; who's going to admire it? Anger throws away his fangs. Fear puts away his chains. Whom can they impress? Finally, the whole cast gives it up as a bad job and goes home. In other words, when you can direct attention, your thinking will never be compulsive again.[5]

Loosening attachment is different than detachment

Loosening attachment to your STUFF does not mean *detaching* from it. The practice of meditation is *not intended* to cultivate qualities of detachment, such as aloofness, indifference, or denial. Meditation is a practice of witnessing and accepting your STUFF rather than becoming indifferent to it or denying it. This subject will be discussed in more detail in Chapter 7.

Gaining perspective, witnessing, and seeing your STUFF clearly and directly

Once your attachment to your STUFF is loosened, you can gain perspective and witness your STUFF directly. It is this perspective—this witnessing—that allows you to see your STUFF clearly rather than become engulfed by it. Seeing your STUFF clearly and directly can help you recognize its nature: it is subjective, habitual, and impermanent. This clear and direct seeing is key to the practice of meditation.

By practicing seeing clearly and directly while you are

meditating, you are training your mind to be able to see more clearly and directly in daily life as well. This awareness can help you to *respond consciously* to life rather than to *react unconsciously.*

Consider this example: A father waits for his teenage daughter to come home; she has missed her curfew again. His imagination is stirred, as it always is when she is late. He might think, *Maybe she's hurt, or maybe she's lost, or maybe she's in trouble.* He's creating stories that in turn, create stress. Here's where meditation comes in to play. If the father meditates regularly, he may be able to loosen his attachment to his STUFF. By stepping back and witnessing his STUFF, he may be able to see it clearly without being engulfed by it—noticing his anxious thoughts as they arise and releasing his stories and their associated stress. He is not denying his STUFF or pushing it away; rather, he is simply noticing it and then making a conscious choice about how to respond to what's happening in the moment.

The clear and direct seeing of your STUFF can diminish its power, just as the power of the wizard in the *Wizard of Oz* was diminished by looking directly at the man behind the curtain. Once the curtain was parted to reveal the truth, the illusion of the Wizard being all-powerful faded away.

Chapter 4 Summary

- *Meditation trains your mind to add space between life and your response to life, allowing you to:*

  - *loosen your attachment to your STUFF and witness it,*

  - *see your STUFF clearly and directly without being engulfed by it, and*

  - *respond consciously to life rather than react unconsciously.*

- *Loosening attachment is different than detachment. Meditation is not a practice of denying or becoming indifferent to your stuff; rather, it is a practice of accepting your stuff and seeing it directly.*

Coming next in Part III: Learn how to meditate, starting with types of anchors in Chapter 5.

PART III

HOW TO MEDITATE

5 ◈ THE ANCHOR

Choosing a neutral object
of awareness

Meditation is practiced by resting your attention on your anchor—your object of awareness. Whenever your attention wanders, gently direct it back to your anchor.

The anchor can take many different forms

There are many different types of anchors, including:

◈ The awareness of your breath moving in and out of your body. The breath is one of the most common anchors—always available, convenient, and accessible.

- ✑ Sounds, including sounds of the forest, ocean, or singing birds. You can even use the sound of traffic as an anchor—just not while driving!

- ✑ A word or phrase (sometimes called a mantra) repeated silently to yourself with each breath. Examples are "peace," or "love," or "light." Alternatively, you can use one word or phrase for your inhale and a different one for your exhale, for example, "breathing in peace, breathing out release." A word or phrase from poetry or your faith tradition can also be used.

- ✑ A visual anchor—such as a candle—that you gaze upon softly.

- ✑ A tactile anchor, such as a smooth stone or a string of prayer beads.

- ✑ The awareness of your body as you notice your immediate physical experience of movements or sensations.

The anchor should be neutral so that it does not create more STUFF

The anchor is considered to be neutral; it should not distract you with its meaning. By using a neutral anchor, your awareness is resting on something that will not generate more STUFF.

If you use the awareness of sound as your anchor, repetitive sound could work well. For example, you could rest your attention on the vibration of the sounds of recorded chanting or ocean waves as they become louder and quieter. However, if you use sound that holds meaning for you, such as a favorite song, the anchor would not be as effective, since it could elicit thoughts and feelings. (*I remember when we danced to this song!*)

If you use a word or phrase as your anchor, it would be considered neutral if you could rest your attention on the silent repetition of the word or phrase without being distracted by its meaning. For instance, if you use the word "love" as your anchor, it would not be effective if it elicited thoughts about love. (*I will always love her!*)

If you use a visual anchor, a candle could work well, while a photo, depending on its subject, has the potential to trigger thoughts and feelings. (*That was the best vacation ever!*)

The awareness of your body would be considered neutral as long as your focus is on the immediate experience (*I notice some tightness in my neck*) but not if you add meaning to the experience (*I notice tightness in my neck. This must be from my car accident. I have to call the doctor and make an appointment. I hope this can get resolved soon!*).

The purpose of the anchor

Essentially, your anchor is a mental tool that is used to direct your attention—to keep it from being tossed about by waves of STUFF in the stream of consciousness.

The anchor gives your mind something to do. Just as a baby can become restless if she doesn't have something to play with, the mind can become agitated if it doesn't have something to do. So in meditation you give your mind just one thing to do—gently focus on your anchor. Your anchor helps loosen your attachment to your STUFF and offers you a resting place for your attention.

Chapter 5 Summary

- ✍ *The anchor is an object of awareness that can take many forms, the most common of which is the breath.*

- ✍ *The anchor should be neutral so that it does not create more* STUFF.

- ✍ *The anchor offers you a resting place for your attention.*

Coming next: Learn how to meditate with an anchor in Chapter 6.

6 ⌒ HOW TO USE AN ANCHOR AS A MEDITATION TOOL

Beginning to practice meditation

Here is an overview of the steps to take for meditation practice. More details on practicing meditation, including illustrations of sitting meditation postures, can be found in Chapter 12.

Choose one anchor for your meditation period. For example, the anchor could be awareness of breath, a word, sounds, or a tactile anchor, such as a smooth stone. Your anchor is your meditation tool.

Set a timer to signal the end of your meditation period. Between 5 and 20 minutes is a good starting point, although those new to meditation may want to start with 5 or 10 minutes and gradually increase their time with continued practice.

Sit on a chair or a floor cushion, keep your spine straight (but not rigid) and your head and neck aligned with your spinal column. Rest your hands on your thighs or lap, and gently close your eyes. This is the position you will maintain during your practice session. (If you are using a visual anchor, or if you would prefer open eyes, keep your eyes open with a soft gaze.)

Spend a few moments or longer bringing awareness to your body. Try to release any physical tension, noticing the points where you make contact with your seat and the ground beneath you and allowing your body to relax into these points. Try to keep your body relaxed but your mind alert. (The body awareness meditations in Chapter 14 offer more details on developing awareness of physical tension.)

Next, place all your attention on your anchor. For example, if your breath is your anchor, place all your attention on the awareness of the breath moving in and out of your body. Notice any qualities of your breathing, such as your chest rising and falling or the coolness of the breath as you inhale and its warmth when you exhale. If a word is your anchor, place all your attention on the word as you silently repeat it, gently focusing on the word as it fills your awareness. If a sound is your anchor, notice its qualities, such as its vibration or the changes in its volume or pitch. If a smooth stone is your anchor, notice its characteristics, such as its shape or temperature.

As much as you can, try to become aware of when your attention wanders away from your anchor. Sometimes your attention will wander and you may not notice that you have become distracted if you are caught up in thought. That's okay. Be gentle with yourself. Once you realize your attention has wandered, gently return it to your anchor.

"Gently" returning your attention to your anchor refers to approaching your meditation practice with acceptance, balance, and compassion—acceptance for your wandering mind and thoughts, balance between trying too hard and not trying at all, and the compassion to meet whatever arises with kindness. (More information on bringing these qualities to your practice can be found in Chapter 8.)

For the remainder of your session, continue with the practice of resting your attention on your anchor, noticing each time your attention wanders, and gently returning it to your anchor. This practice can be challenging for those new to meditation, but like learning any new skill, continued practice is key.

Chapter 6 Summary

- ✑ *Choose your anchor and the length of your meditation period.*

- ✑ *Settle into your meditation position, bring awareness to your body, and try to release any physical tension. Try to keep your body relaxed but your mind alert.*

- ✑ *Rest your attention on your anchor.*

- ✑ *Notice every time your attention wanders, and gently return your attention to your anchor.*

- ✑ *Detailed instructions on practicing meditation can be found in Chapter 12.*

Coming next: Learn why distractions are part of the practice in Chapter 7.

7 ✎ THE MEDITATION MYTH

Recognizing the nature of meditation

Meditation is a simple process, as you can see from the steps in the previous chapter. The practice does not require any fancy gear or equipment. All you need to do is gently focus your attention on your anchor. So why does meditation seem so challenging to some? Why do so many people say they fail at the practice? Because of the "Meditation Myth."

MEDITATION MYTH: Meditation is about stopping all thoughts and feelings.

TRUTH: Meditation is about coming into the here and now with awareness.

Although many people think the practice of meditation involves stopping all thoughts and feelings, this is not so. Expect that thoughts and feelings will continue to arise.

Meditation is a practice of returning to your immediate experience in the present moment. Again and again and again. *Notice* when your attention wanders, and then *return* your attention to your anchor. This process is key to the practice of meditation, since it exercises your mind's "muscle." Just as the repetitive motion of abdominal exercises can build your core strength, the repetitive noticing and returning can build your awareness.

If you are dealing with difficult feelings that arise repeatedly, that's okay. Just notice your immediate experience. You could even direct your awareness to the feeling in your body (for example, noticing tightness in your shoulders) before returning to awareness of your anchor. Meditation is not about suppressing thoughts and feelings; rather, it is a process of noticing them without adding more STUFF to them. Do not deny, resist, or suppress the STUFF that runs through your mind.

Consider the story about a new meditation practitioner who, after her first 20 minutes of meditation, lamented to her wise teacher, "I'm such a failure at this. In 20 minutes I've had 10,000 thoughts!" Her teacher replied, "How lovely! Ten thousand opportunities to return to the present moment."[6]

Chapter 7 Summary

- ✑ *Meditation is not a practice of stopping thoughts and feelings.*

- ✑ *Do not deny, resist, or suppress the wanderings of the mind.*

- ✑ *Expect that thoughts and feelings will continue to arise.*

- ✑ *If you are dealing with difficult feelings that arise repeatedly, that's okay.*

- ✑ *Notice each time your STUFF arises, release it, and gently return your attention to your anchor.*

Coming next: Learn about additional ways meditation can train your mind in Chapter 8.

8 ⟆ THE ABCs OF MEDITATION
Cultivating positive qualities

In addition to cultivating awareness, meditation can cultivate many other positive qualities. As much as you can, begin your meditation time with the intention of bringing acceptance, balance, and compassion to your practice.

Acceptance is the capacity to release judgments and accept what arises. If you resist thoughts, the resistance itself will add more thoughts to your mind. For instance, if a thought arises (*I wonder if we can maintain our relationship?*) and then you judge it (*Oh no, I shouldn't be thinking about that again, especially now while I'm trying to meditate!*), the judgment itself will generate STUFF with an emotional charge. Try instead to be a neutral observer. (*I notice I'm thinking about the relationship again.*) Accept what arises and then gently come back to awareness of your anchor.

Balance is finding the middle ground between directing attention to the anchor with maximum effort and not directing attention to the anchor at all. Just as musicians try to balance the tension of their guitar strings between too strained and too slack, meditators try to balance the quality of their attention in the same way.

Compassion is the capacity to meet whatever arises with kindness. If you notice thoughts about yourself that are not compassionate, see if you can bring a sense of kindness to yourself, if even for your own imperfections. If you notice thoughts about others that are not compassionate, see if you can bring a sense of kindness to others, if even for their imperfections. If you notice you are having difficulty releasing thoughts that are not compassionate, see if you can bring a sense of kindness to the difficulty itself. The practice of compassion in meditation may actually reduce stress and enhance well-being.[7]

Remember the ABCs of meditation: acceptance, balance, and compassion. Cultivating these qualities can bring more peace into your daily life.

Chapter 8 Summary

   Remember to practice the ABCs of meditation:

      acceptance,

      balance, and

      compassion.

   Meeting whatever arises in meditation with these qualities can help you embody these qualities in daily life.

Coming next: Discover images that can support your practice in Chapter 9.

9 ᴁ IMAGES TO SUPPORT YOUR MEDITATION PRACTICE

Illuminating the practice of meditation with images

To understand the practice of meditation, consider any one of the following images:

Imagine sitting on the bank of a flowing stream, watching your STUFF float by without being swept downstream along with it. Anytime your attention *is* swept downstream, come back to your anchor. Your anchor is your resting place. Simply allow your STUFF to flow past, down the stream (of consciousness).

Imagine your STUFF like clouds floating through your mind. Let the clouds pass as you rest your awareness on your breath.

Imagine you are in a crowded restaurant trying to talk with a friend. The loud conversation from another table keeps pulling your attention away. But you keep refocusing on your friend. Your friend is your anchor.

Listen to your thoughts as if you were listening to chattering birds—hearing the chattering without giving it meaning and then letting it fade into the background.

Shift the focus of your awareness from the activity of your mind to the qualities of your heart, such as love and compassion.

Imagine your head as a balloon with a knot tied at your neck. Untie the knot, and allow your consciousness to flow into your body.

Let the spaces amidst your STUFF become more expansive, just as the rings made by a skipping stone on a lake's surface become wider and wider.

Like the settling snowflakes in a snow globe after it's been shaken, allow the energy of your STUFF to gently settle down.

Picture your mind like the surface of a lake or of the ocean. In his book *Wherever You Go, There You Are*, meditation teacher Jon Kabat-Zinn uses this image to describe awareness of the present moment, also known as mind-fulness.

One way to envision how mindfulness works is to think of your mind as the surface of a lake or of the ocean. There are always waves on the water. Some-times they are big, sometimes they are small, and sometimes they are almost imperceptible. The water's waves are churned up by winds, which come and go and vary in direction and intensity, just as do the winds of stress and change in our lives, which stir up waves in our minds.... But just as you can't put a glass plate on the water to calm the waves, so you can't artificially suppress the waves of your mind, and it is not too smart to try. It will only create more tension and inner struggle, not calmness. That doesn't mean that calmness is unattainable. It's just that it cannot be attained by suppressing the mind's natural activity... The spirit of meditation practice was nicely captured on a poster of a seventy-ish yogi, Swami Satchitananda, in full white beard and flowing robes atop a surfboard riding the waves off a Hawaiian beach. The caption read: "You can't stop the waves, but you can learn how to surf."[8]

Chapter 9 Summary

- *The practice of meditation can be understood through images, such as:*

  - *watching your* STUFF *float down your stream of consciousness,*

  - *imagining* STUFF *like passing clouds in the sky, and*

  - *imagining your mind like the surface of a lake or of the ocean.*

Coming next in Part IV: Learn how to apply skills from practice to daily life, starting with easily accessible practices in Chapter 10.

PART IV

FROM PRACTICE TO DAILY LIVING

10   INCORPORATING NEW SKILLS INTO DAILY LIFE

Extending meditation practices into everyday living

There are always opportunities to apply the skills learned in meditation practices into daily life. Easily accessible practices include the following:

Untangling psychological stress from physical stress

When mental stress arises, physical stress often follows. Muscles tighten, breathing becomes restricted, and soon the physical and mental responses team up, wielding much power.

An "untangling" can occur by developing awareness of mental tension and muscular tension as two distinct responses. The stress response loses some of its power when these two forces are not teamed together as one. (The body awareness meditations in Chapter 14 can help you develop awareness of physical tension.)

Consider the following situation: While at the dentist, a man becomes aware of negative thoughts. (*I don't like being here!*) He directs his awareness to his body and notices tension everywhere, as if he is ready to fend off the worst experience imaginable. What would happen if he releases the muscular tension? (*Ah—much better.*) The negative thoughts still remain, but when they're not joined with a physical stress response, the experience becomes more manageable.

Bringing awareness to your body as you walk

Walking from one point to the next offers you an opportunity to take a meditation break. Here's an example: While a man is getting ready for a big presentation at work, his accountant calls to say he owes thousands of dollars in taxes. He is overcome with a whirlwind of emotion. Yet knowing that he needs to focus for his upcoming presentation, he decides to practice a walking meditation. He begins a process of walking mindfully down the corridor of his office building, noticing where his feet connect with the ground. He becomes aware of feelings each time they arise, then shifts his awareness back to his feet. He still has many mixed emotions, but the practice of shifting his awareness to his feet helps him feel more balanced and centered. (Instructions for walking meditation can be found in Chapter 14.)

Using awareness of the breath to reduce stress

The breath is always available, convenient, and accessible. Taking a moment to focus on the breath can reduce stress. Consider this situation: A woman collapses and gashes her chin, so her husband rushes her to the hospital. As they wait for the plastic surgeon, her thoughts race. (*How long will we be here? Who is the doctor? Will my face be okay? Will I be okay?*) When the doctor finally arrives and begins his preparations, she finds herself scrutinizing his actions, and her mind continues to churn.

Just as her racing thoughts are about to take control, she remembers to focus on her breath. Every time another anxious thought arises, she notices the thought, releases it, and returns her awareness to the rhythmic rising and falling of her breath. This practice reduces her stress and reminds her to stay connected to her immediate experience—rather than lost in questions about the future.

Chapter 10 Summary

- *Meditation practices can be incorporated into daily living.*

- *Practices that are easily accessible include:*

  - *untangling mental stress from physical stress,*

  - *bringing awareness to your body as you walk, and*

  - *using awareness of your breath to reduce stress.*

Coming next: Learn about the practice of "not knowing" in Chapter 11.

11 ✎ ENTERING THE PRESENT MOMENT

Choosing to move into a space of "not knowing"

The present moment can be a place of not knowing

The practice of meditation trains the mind to rest in the immediacy of the present moment. Upon entering this moment, one can let go of past stories and imagined future stories—both of which give the illusion of a sense of control—and enter a space of *not knowing*.

The father waiting for his teenage daughter *didn't know* why his child was late; he only knew that she was late. The woman in the hospital emergency room *didn't know* the outcome; she only knew she needed medical attention. Both individuals called on their meditation practices to remain in the immediate experience of the present moment rather than lost in anxiety of imagined future outcomes.

"Not knowing" is different than "not planning"

Entering the space of *not knowing* is different than not planning. One can plan for the future without getting lost in anxiety about imagined future outcomes and without trying to "control" the future. People can control their actions, but they cannot control the results.

The practice of "not knowing"

"Not knowing is most intimate" is an important concept in meditation practice. Intimacy in this sense means the direct awareness that brings you closer to both the immediacy of the present moment and to your true self. By not imagining outcomes based on fears, judgments, memories, and the like, you can remain open and present to *what is*.

Consider the following scenario: A woman takes a taxi to the airport in near-blizzard conditions. Snow falls steadily, and cars spin out of control, yet she remains in a space of "not knowing" and remains calm about what will happen next. *Will the car spin out? Will they get into an accident?*

Will she miss her flight? As each anxious thought begins to arise, she reminds herself that she doesn't know, and the thought loses its power.

She only knows for certain that snow is falling and accumulating, and drivers are struggling with poor road conditions. She finds it freeing to notice her stories without getting lost in them—and instead, live in the immediacy of the present moment.

She simply notices when she wants to make an assumption about the future, and then she reminds herself that she doesn't know. If you could listen to her thoughts, you might hear: *Will I get to the airport? I don't know. Will the weather be okay to fly? I don't know.*

Being comfortable with not knowing can bring enormous freedom and with it, awareness of the moment as it really is.

Moving into not knowing takes courage

It can take courage to let go of your STUFF and the illusion of control—and instead, move into a space where you simply don't know.

The ancient mystic poet Rumi wrote of moving into the unknown. Here's a translation by Coleman Barks, the premier English interpreter of Rumi:

Think how it is to have a conversation with an embryo.
You might say, "The world outside is vast and intricate.
There are wheat fields and mountain passes,
and orchards in bloom.

At night there are millions of galaxies, and in sunlight
the beauty of friends dancing at a wedding."

You ask the embryo why he, or she, stays cooped up
in the dark with eyes closed.

 Listen to the answer.

There is no "other world."
I only know what I've experienced.
You must be hallucinating.[9]

Spiritual teacher and author Harold Kushner also spoke
of moving into the unknown when asked what happens after we die. He said he couldn't possibly describe what happens next—if he did know what was next, it would be like
a child who wasn't born yet "knowing that in ten months
from now she would be wearing red sneakers and watching
television."[10]

We simply don't know what the future holds. Each
breath is a new beginning and a new ending. Staying in
the immediacy of the present moment can be challenging,
but it can be realized with practice. Sometimes the practice is simply one of remembering to focus on just this
next breath. And then the next one. And so on...

Chapter 11 Summary

⇝ *By fully embracing the present moment, you can enter a space of not knowing.*

⇝ *Being comfortable with not knowing can bring enormous freedom—and awareness of the moment as it really is.*

⇝ *Moving into not knowing takes courage.*

Coming next in Part V: Learn how to prepare for meditation, how to approach "obstacles" to meditation—and discover 21 different meditation practices.

PART V

**MEDITATION
PRACTICE**

🌿 INTRODUCTION TO MEDITATION
   PRACTICE

Just as your electronic devices need recharging, so do you. Time spent in meditation is time spent recharging your body, mind, and spirit. Unlike doing abdominal crunches where you can immediately feel results when you exercise, meditation takes time and patience. But if you stick with it, the fruits of the practice can be plentiful. As an old saying goes, "You can't pull up a flower to make it grow faster, but watering it regularly will help it flourish."

Many people new to meditation are surprised by the amount of STUFF they notice. Some report that meditation is quite challenging, even for short periods of time. Start with a manageable amount of time, even for a few minutes each day. Once you become more experienced, you will likely find you are able to increase your meditation time.

You'll find a variety of meditation practices in Part V.

You can try a different one each time you meditate, or stay with a favorite practice. Any of these practices can be adapted to fit your needs.

Chapter 12 discusses getting ready to meditate. This is the preparation for the practices in subsequent chapters.

Chapter 13 offers strategies for addressing common "obstacles" to meditation.

Chapter 14 offers practices that focus awareness. This type of meditation uses an anchor as a focal point for your awareness.

Chapter 15 offers practices that cultivate specific qualities. These meditations focus on developing attributes that can enhance your life.

All of these meditations can either be read *by* you, or read *to* you by someone else as you practice. You can also record any meditation, allowing a bit of space between each instruction, and play it during your practice period. Additionally, as of June 2013, readers can find a free audio guided meditation on: http://www.meditationilluminated.com.

Please note: Meditation should not be practiced while driving or while engaged in any other activity that requires your attention.

12 ✎ GETTING READY TO MEDITATE
Finding time to practice

Finding time to practice is essential, as the following story illustrates: A man once approached a meditation teacher and asked him how he could find peace of mind. The teacher suggested the man take time every morning and evening to meditate. The man exclaimed, "But I don't have time to do that! I'm a very busy man!" He pulled out his smartphone. "Look at all these emails I have to respond to! Please, suggest a much easier path."

The teacher replied, "Okay, then try to practice just once a day for ten minutes."

"But I don't have enough free time to do even that!" the man exclaimed. "Isn't there an easier way?"

"How far is it from the desk in your office to the water cooler?" asked the teacher.

Puzzled by the strange question, the businessman said, "About 30 feet."

"I'm sure you're not working when you walk to the water cooler. So try focusing on your breath when you go to get a drink of water."

The next day at work, the man remembered to focus on his breathing as he walked to the water cooler. As he walked to lunch, he realized he could focus on his breathing as well. In fact, he realized he could rest his awareness on his breath many times throughout the day. As the days progressed, he found more opportunities to focus on his breath until it became a habit—and he finally discovered some peace of mind.[11]

Choose a dedicated place to meditate

You can learn to associate a dedicated place with quieting your mind. Meditating in the same place can help support your practice. Your place could even be a portable place—for example, a meditation cushion that you use in different settings. You could devote an entire room to meditation, or just a corner of a room. One meditator carved out a small space next to the dryer in her basement laundry room. Installing a sliding translucent screen for an outer wall transformed this basement nook into a sacred space. Another transformed a bedroom corner into a private meditation space by using a sheer curtain as a divider. Another uses a favorite chair in the living room.

A meditation place should include a dedicated place to sit, such as a chair or meditation cushion, and could also include inspirational items, such as books of short readings (for before or after your practice), meditation beads, candles, or audio recordings.

Schedule practice

One way to establish a regular routine for your practice is to meditate at the same time each day. Some people schedule their practice times in their calendars. A practice session of 20–30 minutes every day, or almost every day, is preferable, though beginning meditators may want to choose a shorter meditation period. Practicing daily for short periods (even 5–10 minutes) is more beneficial than practicing less regularly for longer periods.

If you are unable to schedule time on a daily basis, practice when you can. Since part of the discipline of meditation is to cultivate acceptance and compassion, consider adopting these qualities if you can't schedule as much practice as you think you "should." Some practice is better than no practice at all.

Settle into your practice session

Your clothing should be comfortable and allow you to breathe freely.

Choose the type of meditation you will be practicing and the length of your practice session. Set any type of timer to signal the end of the session. You can even purchase a special meditation timer with a soft ring (available through many online sources).

Start your practice by remembering the ABCs of meditation: acceptance, balance, and compassion. Try to meet whatever arises with these qualities.

Sit in your meditation position

Sit in a comfortable posture that you can maintain for your practice time. If you are sitting on a chair, sit with your feet shoulder-width apart, as in Illustration 1. (In this position, it is preferable to have your feet flat on the ground. If they do not reach the ground, props such as yoga blocks can be used under your feet.) You can also sit on a chair or floor cushion in a comfortable cross-legged position, one example of which is in Illustration 2. Rest your hands on your thighs or lap.

Keep your spine straight and your head and neck aligned with your spinal column.

Lower your eyelids without changing the position of your head and neck. Keeping your eyes fully closed helps reduce visual stimulation. If you prefer to keep your eyes open, gaze softly at the ground, with lids partially lowered. Keep your eyes softly opened, as well, to use a visual anchor (such as a candle), or for walking meditation, as described in Chapter 14.

You are now in your meditation position—the position to maintain during your practice session.

Seated meditation posture on a chair (Illustration 1)

Seated meditation posture on a cushion (Illustration 2)

Maintain a standardized hand position

A standardized hand position can be an association for relaxation. As your hands rest on your thighs or lap, position them either palms up or palms down. Allow your fingers to relax and curl naturally. Alternatively, lightly touch your right index finger tip to the tip of your right thumb, and touch your left index finger tip to the tip of your left thumb. Another widely-used hand position is one where the dominant hand rests palm up in your lap and the other hand rests palm up on top of the dominant hand, with the thumbs lightly touching to form an oval.

Start with body awareness

Once you are settled in your seat, bring your awareness to your body. Meditation is more accessible when you move from awareness of the gross form (body) to awareness of the subtle form (mind). It's easier to control the body than to control the mind, since your body responds to your instructions more readily than your mind does. For example, your body will walk more slowly if you tell it to, but telling your mind to think more slowly will not often work.[12]

Notice your breath for a few moments or longer, and become aware of the pace of your breathing without changing it. Just notice your breathing as it is. Notice your belly expanding and filling with air as you inhale. Allow your belly to release with your exhale. You can even rest your hand on your belly to feel it rise and fall with each inhale and exhale.

Next, take a few moments or longer to notice the points where you make contact with your seat and the ground beneath you. Try to allow your body to relax into these points of contact. Allow the seat and the ground beneath you to support you, and allow your spine to support you.

Try to release any muscle that is not being used to support you, and allow gravity to help you release towards the earth. You don't need to hold on to anything; simply allow your muscles to let go. Try to keep your body relaxed but your mind alert.

If you'd like further instruction on releasing physical tension, please refer to either the Body Scan Meditation or the Progressive Muscle Relaxation described in Chapter 14.

13 🍂 STRATEGIES FOR ADDRESSING COMMON "OBSTACLES" TO MEDITATION

There are no obstacles—there are only opportunities

If you are wondering why the word *obstacles* is in quotation marks in the chapter title, it is because many experiences that might be considered obstacles to meditation actually offer opportunities to practice. Meditation practice is not about creating a pleasant diversion for yourself—it is about developing awareness. No matter what arises, you have an opportunity to practice noticing.

Here are strategies to address common experiences in meditation.

Busy mind

Although many think a busy mind is an obstacle, this is simply not so, as explained in Chapter 7, "The Meditation Myth." Whether you have the same thoughts and feelings cycling through your mind, or whether you experience a steady stream of different thoughts and feelings, see if you can accept the wanderings of the mind. Awareness of your STUFF can actually be an effective tool to remind you to return your awareness to your anchor. The quality of your awareness is more important than the quantity of your STUFF.

Sleepiness

As the body begins to relax, sleepiness can often arise. You can use the sleepiness itself as your object of awareness, noticing the sleepiness, and then shifting your attention back to your anchor. You can also try to meditate with your eyes slightly open with a soft gaze, since you're unlikely to fall asleep with open eyes. Sitting forward away from back support can also help you stay awake. Alternatively, try a walking meditation, as described in Chapter 14.

Restlessness

The opposite of sleepiness, restlessness arises when you have too much energy, making it difficult to settle down. You can use the restlessness itself as your object of awareness. Where do you feel it in your body? (*For example, can you notice any parts of your body that feel jittery?*) Can you notice the restlessness in your mind? (*For example, are your thoughts jumping around so much that it seems difficult to try to settle down?*) Can you untangle the sensations in your body from the STUFF in your mind and recognize their distinct qualities? Try to note where you sense your restlessness, and then refocus on your anchor. Whenever your restlessness captures your attention, repeat the process of noting your restlessness and refocusing on your anchor.

Alternatively, meditations that focus on the body (for example, the progressive muscle relaxation and walking meditations described in Chapter 14) offer your body something to do, giving your restlessness an outlet.

Boredom

The practice of meditation can seem tedious at times, and feelings of boredom may arise. See if you can notice boredom each time it arises, and return your attention to your anchor. The boredom will likely change with continued practice. Remember, feelings are not permanent.

Physical discomfort

Once you get settled into your meditation position, try to make as few adjustments as possible to reduce fidgeting, a form of physical restlessness and a distraction. If something is causing mild physical discomfort (for instance, an itch), try to sit with the unease for just a moment before making an adjustment; the discomfort may change or go away on its own. Sometimes imagining your breath traveling to the area of discomfort can help release it. If the discomfort continues, bring all your attention to making a gentle adjustment; for that moment, treat the adjustment itself as your object of awareness.

Discomfort with silence

If you are not used to being silent, it can be uncomfortable at first. However, people commonly find that they get used to silence and enjoy it after continued practice. Alternatively, try a sound meditation using chanting or other recorded sound, as described in Chapter 14.

Not practicing

The benefits of meditation come through regular practice. If you find you are not practicing, consider making adjustments so you are more likely to practice—for instance, scheduling shorter, manageable practice sessions or changing the time of day you meditate. Many people find that meditating immediately upon arising in the morning is a good way to fit practice into a busy schedule. Reaping the rewards of the practice may take some time, but most people find the time is well worth it.

Opportunities to Practice

Any experience that arises could be seen as an opportunity to deepen your practice. Meeting experiences with a friendly attitude can open the door to new learning.

14 ✎ MEDITATIONS WITH FOCUSED AWARENESS

The following meditations use an anchor as a focal point for your awareness. You will find instructions for each of them within this chapter. Although many of the meditations begin the same way, they are all different from one another.

Body

> Body Scan Meditation
> Progressive Muscle Relaxation
> Standing Body Awareness Meditation

Breath

> Counting Breath Meditation
> Basic Breath Awareness Meditation
> Continued Breath Awareness Instructions

Words

Meditation with a Word or Phrase I
Meditation with a Word or Phrase II

Awareness of STUFF

Labeling Meditation
Meditation on Spaciousness

Movement

Walking Meditation
Alternative Walking Meditation
Walking Meditation with a Labyrinth

Sound

Sound Meditation

Touch

Stone Meditation I

Body Scan Meditation

The Body Scan Meditation helps you become aware of physical tension so you can begin to release it. Your anchor for this meditation is your body. If you notice tense areas that won't release, try to meet them with an attitude of acceptance. Practice for as little as 1 or 2 minutes to 20 minutes or longer. Use this as a stand-alone practice or as a starting point for any other meditation.

Sit in your meditation position, and start with body awareness as described on pages 76–77.

This meditation uses a process of focusing on one muscle group at a time. Take as much time as needed with each group before moving on to the next one.

Pay attention to any tense areas of your body to try to release them. One way to release tension is to imagine your inhale traveling to the area of tension and surrounding it, and then imagine gently releasing the tension with your exhale. Another way to release tension is to imagine any tense areas getting warmer and warmer until they melt away. You also could imagine any tensed muscles just relaxing and releasing.

Starting with your head, bring your awareness to your forehead and to your eyes, and imagine the area between your eyes getting wider as you gently release any tightened muscles.

Bring your awareness to your cheeks and jaw. Do you notice any tension? Let your jaw be slack. You may want to part your lips the tiniest bit—so that they are barely touching each other. Try to release any tension here.

Bring your awareness to your shoulders and neck. If you can, gently shrug your shoulders up to your ears—and then gently release them, and let them drop. Try to release any tension here.

Bring your awareness to your upper chest and upper back. Notice how this area expands and contracts with each breath. Try to release any tension.

Bring your awareness to your abdomen and mid back, and notice how this area expands and contracts with each breath. Try to release any tension.

Bring your awareness to your low back, hips, and buttocks where you connect with your seat. Try to release any tension.

Bring your awareness to your thighs, knees, calves, and feet. Allow the whole lower portion of your body to be heavy, noticing where you connect with your seat and with the ground. Try to release any tension.

Finally, bring your awareness to your entire body, and notice any areas that still may feel tense or tight. See if you can release any more tension.

Throughout this process, be aware of your body and how it feels. Allow your spine to support you, and allow the seat and ground beneath you to support you. Release any muscles not needed to support you. Keep your body relaxed but your mind alert.

These instructions are a synthesis of meditation teachings from different traditions.

Progressive Muscle Relaxation

The Progressive Muscle Relaxation meditation offers an active way to release physical tension. Your anchor for this meditation is your body. Practice for as little as 1 or 2 minutes to 20 minutes or longer.

This meditation can be used either to develop body awareness, or, alternatively, it can be practiced lying down to help you relax and fall asleep. Each muscle group is tightened and released to help you differentiate between what a muscle feels like when it's tensed versus what it feels like when it's relaxed. This awareness can help you notice tense muscles and learn how to relax them.

Spend as much time as you'd like focusing on each muscle group. You may want to remove your shoes so you can easily curl your toes during the foot relaxation segment.

Pay close attention to your physical comfort. Do not continue with any instruction if it causes discomfort of any kind. Modify as necessary for your body's needs.

Sit in your meditation position, and start with body awareness as described on pages 76–77. (If you are using this meditation to prepare for sleep, lie down on your bed in a comfortable position.)

Begin by focusing on your breath. Notice the pace of your breathing without changing it. Notice the length of your inhale and the length of your exhale. Notice your chest rising and falling with each breath you take. Take a few minutes (or longer) to focus on your breath before moving on to the next step.

Now bring your attention to your feet. Point your feet downward, and curl your toes under, tightening the muscles gently. Don't strain. Notice the tension for a few moments, release, and notice the relaxation. Repeat. Become aware of the difference between the tensed muscles and the relaxed muscles.

Bring your attention to your feet once more, but this time point your feet upward and spread your toes apart, tightening the muscles gently. Don't strain. Notice the tension for a few moments, release, and notice the relaxation. Repeat. Become aware of the difference between the tensed muscles and the relaxed muscles.

Gently tighten the muscles of your calves without straining. Notice the tension for a few moments, release, and notice the relaxation. Repeat. Become aware of the difference between the tensed muscles and the relaxed muscles.

Bring your attention to your thighs, and gently tighten the muscles without straining. Notice the tension for a few moments, release, and notice the relaxation. Repeat. Become aware of the difference between the tensed muscles and the relaxed muscles.

Gently tighten the muscles of your buttocks without straining. Notice the tension for a few moments, release, and notice the relaxation. Repeat. Become aware of the difference between the tensed muscles and the relaxed muscles.

Notice the whole lower portion of your body. Allow it to be heavy with relaxation.

Gently tighten the muscles of your abdomen without straining. Notice the tension for a few moments, release, and notice the relaxation. Repeat. Become aware of the difference between the tensed muscles and the relaxed muscles.

Gently tighten the muscles of your chest and back without straining. Notice the tension for a few moments, release, and notice the relaxation. Repeat. Become aware of the difference between the tensed muscles and the relaxed muscles.

Very gently shrug your shoulders straight up towards your ears without straining. Notice the tension for a few moments, release, and notice the relaxation. Repeat. Become aware of the difference between the tensed muscles and the relaxed muscles.

Gently tighten your fists and the whole length of both arms without straining. Notice the tension for a few moments, release, and notice the relaxation. Repeat. Become aware of the difference between the tensed muscles and the relaxed muscles.

Very, very gently, take a moment to stretch your head and neck front to back and side to side. Become aware of the difference between the tensed muscles and the relaxed muscles.

Tense the muscles of your entire face. Tighten the muscles of your eyes, nose, cheeks and mouth as much as you can. Hold the tension and then release. Repeat. Notice the difference between the tension and the relaxation.

Finally, take a moment to gently stretch your entire body, from the tips of your fingers to the tips of your toes. Release the stretch, and notice the difference between the tension and the relaxation.

Take a moment to scan your entire body, and notice how it feels. Remember the feeling of releasing tension from your muscles, so you can develop a body memory of the sense of relaxation.

The technique of progressive muscle relaxation was developed by American physician Edmund Jacobson in the 1920s.[13]

Standing Body Awareness Meditation

The Standing Body Awareness Meditation can help to develop body awareness, using your body as your anchor. It's a good one to use if you're waiting in line! Practice for as little as 1 or 2 minutes to five minutes or more.

Stand with your feet firmly planted on the ground, hip-distance apart and parallel to each other. Keep your spine, head, and neck aligned. With your eyes softly opened, gently gaze at a point in front of you. Keeping your feet firmly planted, gently rock your body front and back until you find a stable point in the center. Then gently rock side to side until you find a stable point in the center.

Imagine roots growing into the ground from the soles of your feet. Make sure your head and neck are balanced over your spine. See if you can sense strength in your body. You may want to allow yourself to sway a bit like a tree in the wind, so your body does not feel rigid. Focus on your breath without changing the pace of it. Notice your breath moving in and out of your body. Any time your mind wanders, gently bring your attention back to your breath.

This meditation is patterned after instructions commonly given for standing yoga poses.

Counting Breath Meditation

The Counting Breath Meditation uses a combination of counting and awareness of the breath as your anchor. Practice for as little as 1 or 2 minutes to 20 minutes or longer.

Meditation master Thich Nhat Hanh says this practice of counting is like a "string that attaches your mindfulness to your breath."[14]

Sit in your meditation position, and start with body awareness as described on pages 76–77.

Count silently to yourself with each breath. Count *one* as you inhale and count *one* as you exhale. Count *two* on your next inhale, and count *two* again on your next exhale. Count *three* on the following inhale, and count *three* again on the following exhale. Continue counting with each breath through the number ten, then return to the number one. You could also silently say to yourself, "I am inhaling one, I am exhaling one. I am inhaling two, I am exhaling two," etc.

Continue with this counting process. Every time you get to ten, return to one. If at any point during this practice you lose count, simply start over again with the number one.

Continue this practice for the rest of your meditation period.

This meditation is a synthesis of teachings from different traditions, including the teachings of Thich Nhat Hanh.[14]

Basic Breath Awareness Meditation

The Basic Breath Awareness Meditation uses the breath as your anchor. Practice for as little as 1 or 2 minutes to 20 minutes or longer.

Sit in your meditation position, and start with body awareness as described on pages 76–77.

Notice your breath just as it is, and become aware of the pace of your breathing without changing anything. Breathe gently through your nose (if you can), paying attention to your breath either as it enters your nose or flows over your upper lip. Just observe your breathing without trying to change it.

Allow your belly to fill with air and expand with your inhale, and feel it empty and release with your exhale. You can even rest your hand on your belly to feel it rise with your inhale and fall with your exhale.

If you become distracted by anything at all, simply notice the distraction and release it, then gently refocus on your breathing.

See if you can notice the coolness of the air as you breathe in and its warmth as you breathe out.

Notice the length of your inhale and the length of your exhale without changing anything. Just notice.

See if you can notice the pause between each inhale and exhale and between each exhale and inhale.

Try to keep your full attention on just your next breath. And then the next one. And the one after that...

Any time you become distracted by a thought, a feeling, a sound, etc., simply bring your awareness back to your breath. Gently. Without judgment, without internal comment.

Notice your lungs filling and emptying with each inhale and exhale. You can even silently say to yourself *filling, emptying* to help support your experience.

See if you can notice where each breath begins and where each breath ends.

If your attention wanders, begin again. Distractions are part of the practice. Each distraction brings you a new opportunity to begin again, a new opportunity to return to the immediate experience of the present moment.

Continue this practice for the rest of your meditation period.

These instructions are a synthesis of meditation teachings from different traditions.

"Your breathing is your greatest friend. Return to it in all your troubles, and you will find comfort and guidance."

—ANCIENT TEACHER[15]

Continued Breath Awareness Instructions

Here are additional instructions that can be used to help you focus on your breath.

Imagine breathing into a point a couple of inches below your navel, and notice that area expand. Then imagine breathing out from the same point, and notice that area contract.

Become aware of receiving energy on the inhale and releasing tension on the exhale. You could even silently say to yourself *receive, release* with each inhale and exhale.

See if you can notice the space between each inhale and exhale, and notice the space between each exhale and inhale.

Notice your lungs filling and emptying. Filling with the inhale, emptying with the exhale. Filling your body with healing energy with the inhale, letting go of all tension with the exhale. Imagine filling your mind with total awareness of your inhale, and imagine emptying your mind of STUFF with your exhale. Just fill and empty.

Let go of "trying" to breathe, and just let the breath come naturally.

Notice the point on your body (nose, chest, belly, etc.) where you are most aware of your breathing.

Notice the rhythmic nature of your breath—its ebb and flow. Each inhale is a new beginning, and each exhale is a new ending.

These instructions are a synthesis of meditation teachings from different traditions.

Meditation with a Word or Phrase I

The Meditation with a Word or Phrase I uses a word or phrase as your anchor. Rather than choosing a word or phrase ahead of time, see if you can allow one to come into your awareness during the meditation, as described below. Practice for as little as 5 minutes to 20 minutes or longer.

The word or phrase you choose will become a resting place for your awareness and should not distract you with its meaning. The word or phrase is repeated continually and silently to yourself, either repeating the same word or phrase for each breath, or using one word or phrase for the inhale and a different one for the exhale. Examples of words or phrases that can be used are: *peace, light, love, oneness, breathe in peace/breathe out harmony, let it be, present moment, be here now, rest in the now, breathing in life-force/breathing out life-force, come home to the breath, arrive, rising/falling, peace/release.* A word or phrase from nature or from your faith tradition can also be used.

Sit in your meditation position, and start with body awareness as described on pages 76–77.

Bring your awareness to your breath for a few minutes or longer. Each time you become distracted, notice the distraction, and allow it to pass.

Next, invite a short word or phrase to come into your awareness—a word or phrase that represents presence in the here and now. Don't try to make anything happen. See if you can allow a word or phrase to arise freely.

For the rest of your meditation period, gently rest your attention on your word or phrase, silently repeating it again and again. Each time your mind wanders, gently bring your attention back to your word or phrase.

If a word or phrase doesn't come into your awareness, simply use your breath as an anchor.

This meditation is a synthesis of teachings from different traditions.[16]

Meditation with a Word or Phrase II

The Meditation with a Word or Phrase II offers an alternative way to practice using a word or phrase as an anchor. Practice for as little as 5 minutes to 20 minutes or longer.

Find an inspirational passage or reading, such as a reading from poetry or from your faith tradition.

Sit in your meditation position, and start with body awareness as described on pages 76–77.

Read the passage silently to yourself one time. Then read it a second time, and this time listen for a word or phrase that attracts you or catches your attention.

Once you've selected a word or phrase, silently and continually repeat it, allowing it to sink into your heart and mind. Place all your attention on your word or phrase, and every time your mind wanders gently refocus on your word or phrase. (If no word or phrase attracts you, simply use your breath as your anchor.) Spend as long as you'd like with this practice.

You can also read the passage a third time, noticing whether the same word or phrase attracts you or if a new one interests you. Repeat the practice using the previous instructions.

This form of meditation is often described as "chewing" the word or phrase. This practice has also been compared to a cow chewing her cud, because the cow is not thinking about past or future events; she's just chewing—and remaining in the immediacy of the present moment.

This passage, adopted from the Gaelic Runes, can be used for your reading:

Deep peace of the running wave to you,
Deep peace of the flowing air to you,
Deep peace of the quiet earth to you,
Deep peace of the shining stars to you,
Deep peace of the infinite peace to you.[17]

This meditation is based on the ancient meditation practice of Lectio Divina.

Labeling Meditation

The Labeling Meditation helps develop your awareness of the wanderings of the mind by labeling any distractions as they arise. Using your breath as your anchor, name each distraction upon noticing it, and then go back to a focus on your breath. The practice is a perfect example of the saying, "If you can name it, you can tame it." Practice for as little as 1 or 2 minutes to 20 minutes or longer.

Sit in your meditation position, and start with body awareness as described on pages 76–77.

Gently rest your awareness on your breathing. Silently say to yourself "breathing" with each breath. Alternatively, silently say "in" with each inhale and "out" with each exhale.

Whenever you become distracted, silently "label" the distraction, and gently refocus on your breath. For example: If your attention is captured by a sound, label it by silently saying "listening," or "hearing," or even "sound." If your attention is captured by a thought or a plan, label it by silently saying "thinking" or "planning." If a physical sensation captures your attention, label it by silently saying "sensation" or you can label the sensation itself, such as "leg cramp." If your attention is captured by a feeling, label it by silently saying "feeling" or label the feeling itself, for example, "sadness" or "restlessness" or "happiness."

After you silently note the distraction, gently refocus on your breathing. Your internal dialogue might go something like this: *breathing, breathing, thinking, planning, breathing, listening, breathing, breathing, feeling, breathing, thinking…*

This practice can be challenging. Once something captures your attention (e.g., a thought, a sound, a feeling), as long as you notice the shift of attention, the noticing itself helps develop awareness. (If you notice that you are concerned about whether you labeled something correctly, you could even label the concern itself, for example, *worrying* or *judging*. Noticing the distraction is more important than labeling the distraction precisely.)

Try to notice the distraction and label it as soon as it arises or immediately afterwards. Then gently refocus on your breath. Continue with this practice for your entire meditation period.

This meditation is based on instructions commonly offered in Buddhist meditation.

Meditation on Spaciousness

The Meditation on Spaciousness further develops awareness of your STUFF. Your anchor is the space between STUFF as it arises and fades away. Practice for as little as 1 or 2 minutes to 20 minutes or longer.

Sit in your meditation position, and start with body awareness as described on pages 76–77.

Now, see if you can notice any space between one thought or feeling and the next one that arises. Direct your attention to the spaciousness between whatever comes into your awareness. As soon as you notice any thought or feeling, gently release it, and allow it to fade. See if you can find just a moment of space before the next thought or feeling arises. Continue with this practice for the rest of your meditation period.

This meditation is a synthesis of instructions commonly offered for meditation.

"Thoughts of themselves have no substance; let them arise and pass away unheeded. Thoughts will not take form of themselves, unless they are grasped by the attention; if they are ignored, there will be no appearing and no disappearing."

—ANCIENT PHILOSOPHER-POET ASHVAGHOSHA[18]

Walking Meditation

The Walking Meditation is a moving meditation that uses your body as your anchor. It can be practiced indoors or outdoors, for just a few steps or for as long as you'd like.

Rest your attention on the movements of your legs and feet.

Lift your right leg to take a step, and silently say to yourself "lifting." Move your right leg forward, and silently say to yourself "moving." Place your right foot down on the ground, and silently say to yourself "placing," and as you shift the weight onto your right foot, silently say to yourself "shifting." Begin the process again with the left foot: lifting, moving, placing, shifting. The phrase "Let My Peace Show"[19] may help you remember these instructions.

Continue silently repeating these words to yourself with each step. Any time your attention wanders, gently refocus on the words and the movements of your body.

The above instructions are commonly offered for walking meditation.

Alternative Walking Meditation

Alternatively, you can rest your attention on the soles of your feet as they touch the ground, and use this awareness as your anchor. Meditation teacher Thich Nhat Hanh says to "walk as if you are kissing the Earth with your feet."[20]

Walking Meditation with a Labyrinth

The Walking Meditation with a Labyrinth uses an indoor or outdoor labyrinth. Indoor and outdoor labyrinths can be found by checking the "worldwide labyrinth locator" at http://labyrinthlocator.com. Most are free and open to the public.

The labyrinth is an ancient meditation tool. It consists of a single winding path that leads to the center and back out again, and is level with the ground—there are no walls or dividers. Unlike a maze, there are no choices to make about which way to turn. Labyrinths can be made from stones, pavers, tile, painted canvas, or many other materials. Their diameter can range from as little as 12 feet to 50 feet or more.

To walk the labyrinth, start at the beginning of the path, follow the twists and turns to the center, pause, and walk out using the same pathway. A walk typically takes between 20 and 45 minutes.

Simply following the path can help you relax your mind. A sense of time and space may be suspended, allowing you to access clarity and insight. A significant physiological effect is created by the many left-to-right and right-to-left turns on the path, which can help balance the left and right sides of the brain and provide a centering experience.

The Walking Meditation instructions can be used when you walk the labyrinth.

Alternatively, here are other suggestions for your walk:

Walk to the center of the labyrinth as a time of releasing, rest in the center for as long as you'd like, and walk out of the labyrinth as a time of integrating any benefits from your walk.

Bring a question to the labyrinth with the intent of being open to whatever clarity may arise during your walk.

Imagine healing energy surrounding you—mind, body, and spirit—as you walk the labyrinth's path.

The above instructions are commonly offered for walking labyrinths.

Sound Meditation

The Sound Meditation uses sound as an anchor. Any time your attention wanders, gently refocus on the sound. Practice for as little as 1 or 2 minutes to 20 minutes or longer.

This meditation can be practiced indoors or outdoors, using the sounds around you or using a recording. Repetitive, neutral sounds such as recorded chanting or nature sounds work well.

Sit in your meditation position, and start with body awareness as described on pages 76–77.

Gently rest your awareness on the sound of your anchor. Any time your attention wanders, gently bring it back to the sound. Imagine nothing else exists but the sound, as you allow your mind and body to fill with its vibration.

In this meditation the practice is to be fully open to the sound, and release any judgments of liking or disliking the sound. Just allow the vibrations to arise, and notice as they change pitch and volume.

Let go of any effort to make sounds come and go, since they will come and go on their own. The practice is simply to be present to the sound. Thich Nhat Hanh says, "Meditation does not have to be hard labor."[21] This is especially true of sound meditation, since you can hear sound without making any special effort to do so.

Continue this practice for the rest of your meditation period.

This meditation is a synthesis of teachings from different traditions.

Stone Meditation I

The Stone Meditation I uses the feeling of a stone as your anchor. Choose a smooth stone that fits into the palm of your hand. Practice for as little as 1 or 2 minutes to 20 minutes or longer.

Sit in your meditation position, and start with body awareness as described on pages 76–77.

Gently rest your awareness on the stone in your hand. Notice its various characteristics, including:

The weight of the stone in your hand—how heavy or light is it?

The temperature of the stone—how warm or cool is it?

The shape of the stone—is it round or oval, or is it a different shape?

The texture of the stone—is it smooth, or is any part of the surface rough?

How the stone fits into your palm—can your fingers close around it?

How does the stone feel if you hold it lightly or if you hold it more tightly?

Any time your attention wanders, gently bring your awareness back to your stone.

Continue this practice for the rest of your meditation period.

This meditation was created for use with a tangible anchor.

15 ✑ MEDITATIONS TO CULTIVATE SPECIFIC QUALITIES

The following meditations focus on cultivating specific qualities that can enhance your life. You will find instructions for each of them within this chapter. Although many of the meditations begin the same way, they are all different from one another.

For the qualities of strength or connectedness
  Stone Meditation II

For the quality of comfort with the unknown
  Meditation on "Not Knowing"

For the qualities of love and gratitude
  Gratitude Practice

To cultivate positive thought patterns
   Positive Thought Practice

For the quality of compassion
   Compassion Meditation

For new growth
   Ground of Being Meditation

For presence and surrender to the present moment
   Awakening and Surrendering Meditation

For healing
   Healing Light Meditation

For peace
   Imagining Peace Meditation

Stone Meditation II

The Stone Meditation II uses the stone as a symbol of your intent to cultivate a quality of strength or of connectedness to something larger than yourself. Use a smooth stone that fits into the palm of your hand. Practice for as little as 1 or 2 minutes to 20 minutes or longer.

Sit in your meditation position, and start with body awareness as described on pages 76–77.

Gently rest your awareness on the stone in your hand. Every time your attention wanders, gently bring it back to your stone and your intent.

To help cultivate the qualities of strength, focus on the solidity and strength of stone—either the stone in your hand or another form of stone, such as a mountain. Whenever your attention wanders, bring it back to the stone and its quality of solidity and strength. Imagine this strength in your mind and body to help cultivate this quality within your entire being.

To help cultivate the qualities of connectedness, focus on the connection your stone has to the earth. Whenever your attention wanders, refocus on awareness of the stone and its connection to the earth. See if you can imagine this connectedness within your entire being—a connection to the earth and to the interdependent web of life.

Continue with either or both of these practices for the remainder of your meditation period.

This meditation is inspired by the qualities of stone.

Meditation on "Not Knowing"

The Meditation on "Not Knowing" helps to develop comfort with not having the answers. (This practice was introduced in Chapter 11.) Practice for as little as 1 or 2 minutes to 20 minutes or longer.

Sit in your meditation position, and start with body awareness as described on pages 76–77.

Can you imagine a situation where you don't know the outcome, but you might want to know? Perhaps you can envision such a time regarding health, work, a relationship, or another situation.

Close your eyes for a moment, and imagine such a time—from the past, the present, or the future. Imagine a time where you simply don't know, or you didn't know. How does it feel not to know the outcome? What is the experience like for you in mind and body? Can you notice thoughts, feelings, and any physical sensations? Are you comfortable with not knowing, or is there a desire for a predictable result? Spend as much time as you'd like and notice what it's like not to know.

You can also practice "not knowing" in your daily life. Simply notice when you want to make an assumption about an outcome in your life. At that moment just tell yourself *I don't know*. Will you catch that bus? *I don't know, and it's okay not to know.* Will you get that raise? *I don't know, and it's okay not to know.* And so on...

This meditation is based on the Zen Buddhist practice of "not knowing."

Gratitude Practice

Gratitude Practice helps to cultivate the qualities of love and gratitude. Practice for as little as 1 or 2 minutes to 20 minutes or longer.

Sit in your meditation position, and start with body awareness as described on pages 76–77.

Bring your awareness to your breath, and silently say to yourself "love" with each inhale and "gratitude" with each exhale. Simply bring all your awareness to the words and your breath, and rest your attention on them. Any time your mind wanders, gently bring your attention back to the words and your breathing. Spend as long as you'd like on this first part of the practice.

When you feel ready, let go of the words. Imagine a time when you felt love and gratitude towards another living being—perhaps a loved one, a pet, a stranger who offered you a small kindness, or even the trees that grace this earth. Imagine the feelings of love and gratitude welling up in you.

Now, imagine sending these feelings of love and gratitude outward. What does it feel like to send out love and gratitude? Take a couple of minutes to become aware of any images, sensations, or feelings in your body and mind as you send these feelings outward.

Next, imagine a time when you felt love and gratitude being directed towards you, by a parent, a child, a friend, a teacher, a pet or an animal, or perhaps by a stranger smiling warmly. You could even imagine receiving love and gratitude from the subject in a photo or painting who offers a loving gaze outward into the world.

Imagine what it feels like to receive love and gratitude. Take a couple of minutes to become aware of any images, sensations, or feelings in your body and mind as you receive the feelings of love and gratitude.

Now, come back to an awareness of your breath. Try to notice the feelings of love and gratitude with each inhale and exhale, receiving love on the inhale and sending out gratitude on the exhale.

Any time your mind wanders, gently bring it back to your breath moving in and out of your body—and to sending and receiving love and gratitude.

Continue with this practice for the rest of your meditation period.

This meditation is inspired by Buddhist lovingkindness meditations.

Positive Thought Practice

The Positive Thought Practice is designed to cultivate positive thoughts and help free you from negative thought patterns. This meditation can be practiced throughout your day.

The practice involves becoming aware of the thoughts that run through your mind. As soon as you notice a negative thought arising, think a few positive thoughts about the object of your negative thinking.

For instance, as soon as you become aware of a negative thought about a person, think a few positive thoughts about this person. If you were to become aware of thinking, *I don't like the way she talks to me*, you could then think, *I am glad to have her in my life; she's done many favors for me in the past; she's a wonderful cook.*

Use the same practice for a situation. As soon as you become aware of a negative thought about a situation, then think a few positive thoughts about it. If you were to become aware of thinking, *These workplace meetings are so boring*, you could then think, *I am glad to have a good job; I am fortunate to be able to work here; I enjoy being with many of my co-workers.*

Become aware, as much as you are able, of the thoughts that run through your mind as you go about your daily life. As soon as you notice a negative thought, see if you can think a few positive thoughts about the object of your negative thinking.

This meditation can be practiced anywhere and anytime.

This practice was inspired by a hope for more positive awareness in the world.

Compassion Meditation

The Compassion Meditation helps to cultivate the quality of compassion. Practice for as little as 1 or 2 minutes to 20 minutes or longer.

Sit in your meditation position, and start with body awareness as described on pages 76–77.

Bring your awareness to your breath. With each inhale imagine your body and mind filling with compassion—compassion for yourself, your family, friends, community, or for people throughout the world, bonded together simply because we all belong to the human race. Feel the sense of caring envelop you as you breathe. Perhaps you'd like to imagine a loved one, or different loved ones, one after another, holding the image of each in your heart, imagining your compassion for them or their compassion for you.

With each exhale just release. Release tension, and release STUFF. Become empty so that you can fill with compassion on the next inhale.

Fill with compassion on the inhale.

Release and become empty on the exhale.

Just fill and empty. There's nothing to do but fill and empty.

You may want to silently recite these phrases as you are directing compassion towards yourself:

May I be held in compassion,
may I be free,
may I be at peace.

Or you may want to silently recite these phrases as you are directing compassion towards others:

May you be held in compassion,
may you be free,
may you be at peace.

Or you may want to silently recite these phrases as you are directing compassion towards the world community:

May we be held in compassion,
may we be free,
may we be at peace.

Continue this practice for the rest of your meditation period.

This meditation is based on the Buddhist practice of lovingkindness.

Ground of Being Meditation

The Ground of Being Meditation helps to cultivate the "ground of your being" to prepare it for new growth. Practice for as little as 5 minutes to 20 minutes or longer.

This meditation uses the metaphor of tilling the ground of your being. Tilling is the process of turning soil over and cultivating it to welcome new growth. The ground of your being is whatever you imagine it to be—body, mind, or spirit.

Sit in your meditation position, and start with body awareness as described on pages 76–77.

Spend a few minutes focusing on your breath, releasing your STUFF as much as you can.

Next is a process of cultivating the ground of your being to prepare it for new growth and renewal. This process of cultivation, or tilling, is done with the breath.

To begin, the soil must be warm enough to till. Take a couple of minutes to imagine breathing the warmth of the sun into your body. Imagine the breath traveling to your entire body and warming it. Just breathe naturally, moving warmth to different parts of your body with each inhale and exhale, and imagine the ground of your being warming with each breath.

As you inhale, you may want to imagine warm light traveling to your entire body—or just to tense areas of your body. As you exhale, you may want to imagine warmth rising from your body. Simply breathe in warm light, and breathe out rising warmth.

With tilling, it is important to be patient. Do not rush the process. Take your time and breathe gently, warming the soil of the ground of your being.

Accept wherever you are right now. Do not try to change anything or push away parts of yourself. Just gently warm up the ground so it is soft and yielding.

When tilling new ground, the invitation is to gently work your way deeper into the soil to yield a fine seedbed for planting. As you take your next inhale, you may want to imagine breathing light into dark areas. As you take your next exhale, allow any darkness in your soil to loosen and gradually turn over. This is a gentle process.

Rather than pushing away dark areas, embrace them and breathe light into them. They will become the compost to promote new growth. As you prepare your seedbed, trust that the layers of darkness, the rich soil of the compost, will allow new growth to emerge.

Take a couple of minutes to breathe in light as you inhale, and allow the darkness to loosen as you exhale. Light as you inhale; loosen as you exhale.

As you continue with the tilling process, if you can, allow a "seed" of an idea to arise from deep within the ground of your being, an idea to plant in your seedbed, an idea of what you'd like to imbue with life.

As much as you can, let go of your thinking mind, and allow an idea to germinate that's sensed from within. The seed of your idea might hold a quality you'd like to cultivate, or it might represent freedom from a belief that you're ready to relinquish. There is no right or wrong. Take a couple of minutes to be receptive to whatever might arise.

If no idea arises, continue to focus on your breath, imagining light with the inhale, and loosening with the exhale.

Finally, if the seed of an idea does arise, imagine gently planting it in the ground of your being and allowing it to take root.

Whether or not you planted a seed, on your next inhale, breathe in light to allow your seedbed to be nourished, and on your next exhale, sensing the flow of breath, imagine that your seedbed will flourish. Light and nourish with the inhale; flow and flourish with the exhale. Light and nourish; flow and flourish.

This meditation is inspired by nature and the coming of spring.

Awakening and Surrendering Meditation

The Awakening and Surrendering Meditation helps to cultivate presence, and the ability to surrender to the present moment. Practice for as little as 1 or 2 minutes to 20 minutes or longer.

This meditation uses an image of awakening and surrendering to each moment with every inhale and every exhale.

Each breath represents a new beginning and a new ending—an awakening with the inhale and a surrendering with the exhale.

Sit in your meditation position, and start with body awareness as described on pages 76–77.

Bring your awareness to your breath. Can you imagine with each inhale simply opening to the moment and all the possibility it holds? Can you imagine embracing the moment just as it is, without trying to change it, but simply opening to the unknown?

Can you imagine with each exhale, just surrendering to the moment and letting go? Perhaps you can release muscular tension, or old stories that are tightly held, or judgments, or emotions from events long passed.

Embracing the moment just as it is can take courage. Releasing tightly held beliefs can also take courage. Just imagine opening to the moment with your inhale and releasing with your exhale. Awakening with the inhale; surrendering with the exhale.

Continue with this practice for the rest of your meditation period.

This meditation is inspired by a hope for present moment awareness.

Healing Light Meditation

The Healing Light Meditation helps to cultivate healing energy in and around your body. Practice for as little as 1 or 2 minutes to 20 minutes or longer.

Sit in your meditation position, and start with body awareness as described as described on pages 76–77.

Imagine the universe as holding an abundant, infinite amount of healing energy. Imagine that energy as being available to you simply by inhaling. You may want to envision the healing energy as a white or golden light.

Breathe the healing light into a point a couple of inches below your navel. Imagine the light filling this area of your body. Cradle the light in this area, and gently hold it, while you exhale any toxins or waste. Continue with this practice for a couple of minutes or longer.

Now, with each inhale, imagine the light traveling through your whole body and infusing every cell with its healing energy. Allow your cells to soak in this energy. With each exhale, imagine releasing any waste or toxins. Continue with this practice. Breathe in healing light;

breathe out and release. You might even imagine a healing light surrounding your entire body during this practice.

This meditation is inspired by instructions commonly offered for healing meditations.

Imagining Peace Meditation

The Imagining Peace Meditation helps to cultivate the quality of peace. Practice for as little as 1 or 2 minutes to 20 minutes or longer.

Sit in your meditation position, and start with body awareness as described on pages 76–77.

Bring your awareness to your breath. As you take your next inhale, see if you can imagine a time when you experienced peacefulness while you were in community—surrounded by a small group of people, or even by hundreds or thousands of people. Perhaps you were in a stadium, an auditorium, or even among crowds in the great outdoors. See if you can imagine the quality of peacefulness as if you are experiencing it again. Notice where you sense it—in mind, body, or spirit. Take time in silence to reflect. Alternatively, you may want to just sit with a focus on your breath, silently saying "peace" on each inhale and "release" on each exhale.

Next, see if you can imagine a time when you experienced peacefulness when you were with just one other. Perhaps you were with a parent, a child, a spouse, a friend, or even a beloved pet. See if you can imagine that quality of peacefulness as if you are experiencing it again. Notice where you sense it—in mind, body, or spirit. Take time in silence to reflect. Alternatively, you may want to just sit with a focus on your breath, silently saying "peace" on each inhale and "release" on each exhale.

Finally, see if you can imagine a time when you experienced peacefulness when you were in solitude. Perhaps you were surrounded by the beauty of nature, or you were in an inspirational place, or in the presence of great art or music. See if you can imagine that quality of peacefulness as if you are experiencing it again. Notice where you sense it—in mind, body, or spirit. Take time in silence to reflect. Alternatively, you may want to just sit with a focus on your breath, silently saying "peace" on each inhale and "release" on each exhale.

As you go forth, may you continue to hold that quality of peace within you—mind, body, and spirit.

This meditation is inspired by a hope for peace.

ꗃ EPILOGUE

An epilogue generally describes what happens next—after what has been depicted in a book.

What happens next is up to you. To experience the benefits of meditation, the next step is to carve out time for practice, if only for a few minutes each day. Meditation can be challenging at first. Be gentle with yourself. Like learning any new skill, repeated practice is key. Your practice does not have to be perfect, and it does not have to encompass all the information in this book. Find one idea that resonates with you, and start with that one. Build from there. Try to create a new habit by associating a specific time or place with meditating.

Remember, meditation can be practiced in a wide variety of ways. I wish you the freedom to discover the ways that are right for you.

*"True education can never be crammed and pumped from
without; rather it must aid in bringing spontaneously to
the surface the infinite hoards of wisdom within."*

—PARAMHANSA YOGANANDA[22]

APPENDIX ⌒ A BRIEF OVERVIEW OF THE SCIENCE BEHIND THE BENEFITS OF MEDITATION

Below is a brief sampling of scientific findings that demonstrate the positive health effects of meditation, including:

- lower stress levels,
- increased focus and awareness, and
- enhanced positive emotion, learning, and memory.

Lower stress levels

Meditation promotes physiological changes that block the ability of stress hormones to influence the brain and body.[23] Meditation can produce an effect on the body that resembles a class of drugs (beta blockers) used to treat the symptoms of stress-related conditions. These changes invoke a natural relaxation response that is the opposite of the fight-or-flight response to stress.[24]

Increased focus and awareness

During meditation, attention is often focused on a repeated sound, word, or phrase.[24] This activates regions of the brain related to attention and focus. Research suggests that the amount of time spent meditating each day is positively correlated with performance on attentional tasks.[25]

Enhanced positive emotion, learning, and memory

Many regions of the brain contain a substance composed of cell bodies known as gray matter, which assists in routing sensory stimuli to the central nervous system. An area with a higher concentration of gray matter suggests a stronger functional ability in processing and transporting information throughout the brain.[26]

Researchers have found that compared to non-meditating individuals, those who meditate have a higher density of gray matter in multiple brain regions, particularly the hippocampus. This suggests that over time, meditation has the ability to benefit the functionality of activities regulated by the hippocampus: learning, memory, and emotion.[26,27]

Studies of practiced meditators also have shown shrinkage and lesser gray matter density in the amygdala, the portion of the brain that initiates the body's response to stress and plays a key role in emotional memory and reactivity. These findings suggest that meditation may help control unconscious emotional reactions.[26-28]

Studies also found that those who meditated had higher levels of brain function in the left frontal region of the brain, a pattern associated with positive, approach-oriented emotional states.[29]

For more information on studies related to meditation, visit the website of the National Center for Complementary and Alternative Medicine (NCCAM) at the National Institutes of Health (http://nccam.nih.gov/health/meditation).

◢ ENDNOTES

1. Swami Vivekananda, *The Complete Works of Swami Vivekananda* (Volume 1, Raja-Yoga, Chapter VI). Retrieved from http://www.ramakrishnavivekananda.info/vivekananda/volume_1/raja-yoga/pratyahara_and_dharana.htm.

2. William Shakespeare, *The Tragedy of Hamlet, Prince of Denmark* (2.2.251).

3. "Everything That Can Go Wrong Listed," *The Onion*, June 15, 2005. Retrieved from http://www.theonion.com/articles/everything-that-can-go-wrong-listed,1344/. Reprinted by publisher permission.

4. Eric Allenbaugh, "An Old Story Told to me by James Newton," in *Wake-Up Calls: You Don't Have to Sleepwalk through Your Life, Love, or Career!* (New York, NY: Simon & Schuster, 1992), 22. Reprinted by author permission.

5. From *Words To Live By*, by Eknath Easwaran, founder of the Blue Mountain Center of Meditation, copyright 1990, 2005; reprinted by permission of Nilgiri Press, P. O. Box 256, Tomales, Ca 94971, www.easwaran.org.

6. Based on a story by Cynthia Bourgeault, *Centering Prayer and Inner Awakening* (Lanham, MD: Cowley Publications, 2004), 23–24. Reprinted by publisher permission.

7. For information on studies of compassion in meditation visit http://neuroscience.stanford.edu/research/programs/program_info/Ccare_051809_rev1.pdf.

8. Jon Kabat-Zinn, *Wherever You Go, There You Are* (New York, NY: Hyperion, 1994), 30–32. Reprinted by publisher permission.

9. Coleman Barks, *The Essential Rumi* (New York, NY: HarperCollins, 1995), 71. Reprinted by author permission.

10. Harold Kushner, "*Overcoming Life's Disappointments.*" Book Tour, JCC of Greater Washington's 38th Annual Book Festival, Rockville, MD. November 8, 2007.

11. Source unknown.

12. Based on the teachings of Mata Amritanandamayi, Public Lecture, Hyatt Regency Reston, Reston, VA. July 7, 2011.

13. For more information on the technique of progressive muscle relaxation and Dr. Edmund Jacobson, visit http://www.progressiverelaxation.org.

14. Thich Nhat Hanh, *The Miracle of Mindfulness* (Boston, MA: Beacon Press, 2004), 21. Cited with publisher permission.

15. Author unknown. Research shows quote with attributions such as "Buddhist Master," "Oriental Master," "Great Teacher," "Tibetan Sage."

16. "Meditation With a Word or Phrase I" inspired by Tilden Edwards, *Living in the Presence* (New York, NY: HarperCollins, 1987), 41. Cited with author permission.

17. The Unitarian Universalist Association, *Singing the Living Tradition* (Boston, MA: Beacon Press, 1993), 681.

18. Ashvaghosha. Retrieved from http://www.easwaran.org/ 145?thoughts=10/30.

19. This phrase was created by a student in one of Joy Rains' *Meditation Practice* classes.

20. Reprinted from *The Long Road Turns to Joy: A Guide to Walking Meditation* (1996, 2011) by Thich Nhat Hanh with permission of Parallax Press, Berkeley, California, www.parallax .org.

21. Thich Nhat Hanh, *"Living Mindfully, Living Peacefully."* Public Lecture, Warner Theater, Washington D.C. October 25, 2011.

22. Paramhansa Yogananda, *Autobiography of a Yogi* (New York, NY: The Philosophical Library, 1946), 257.

23. A. Mohan, R. Sharma, and R. Bijlani, "Effect of Meditation on Stress-Induced Changes in Cognitive Functions," *Journal of Alternative and Complementary Medicine* 17 (3) (2011): 207–212.

24. H. Benson, "The Relaxation Response," in *Mind Body Medicine: How to Use Your Mind for Better Health*, ed. D. Goleman and J. Gurin (New York, NY: Consumer Reports Book, 1993).

25. D. Chan and M. Woollacott, "Effects of Level of Meditation Experience on Attentional Focus: Is the Efficiency of Executive or Orientation Networks Improved?" *Journal of Alternative and Complementary Medicine*, 13(6) (2007): 651–657.

26. B. K. Hölzel, J. Carmody, M. Vangel, C. Congleton, S. M. Yerramsetti, T. Gard, and S. W. Lazar, "Mindfulness Practice Leads to Increases in Regional Brain Gray Matter Density," *Psychiatry Research: Neuroimaging*, 191 (2010): 36–43.

27. Y. Tang, Y. Ma, J. Wang, Y. Fan, S. Feng, Q. Lu, Q. Yu, D. Sui, M. Rothbart, M. Fan, and M. Posner, "Short-term Med-

itation Improves Attention and Self-Regulation," *Proceedings of the National Academy of Sciences of the United States of America*, 104(43) (2007): 17152–17156.

28. A. Lutz, H. A. Slagter, J. D. Dunne, R. J. Davidson, "Attention Regulation and Monitoring in Meditation," *Trends in Cognitive Sciences*, 12(4) (2008): 163–169.

29. C. Moyer, M. Donnelly, J. Andersson, K. Valek, S. Huckaby, D. Wiederholt, R. Doty, A. Rehlinger, and B. Rice, "Frontal Electroencephalographic Asymmetry Associated with Positive Emotion is Produced by Very Brief Meditation Training," *Psychological Science*, 22 (10) (2011): 1277–1279.

✐ GLOSSARY

ANCHOR: An object upon which you focus your attention during meditation. The anchor should be neutral and not distract you with its meaning. Also called an object of awareness.

MEDITATION: A discipline of training the mind through the practice of awareness.

MEDITATION POSITION: The seated position that is maintained during meditation practice. Most commonly, one is seated on a chair or floor cushion with spine straight, head and neck aligned with the spinal column, hands resting in lap, and eyes softly closed.

MINDFULNESS: Present moment awareness.

OBJECT OF AWARENESS: An object upon which you focus your attention during meditation. The object of awareness should be neutral and not distract you with its meaning. Also called an anchor.

PRACTICE: The actual discipline of meditation, a specific exercise in meditation, or the actual practicing of meditation.

STUFF: The content that runs through the mind—Stories, Thoughts, Urges, Frustrations, Feelings.

✐ ACKNOWLEDGMENTS

To my dear friends and family: This book was ushered into being by a group of friends and family who carefully read the manuscript at various stages and offered their different perspectives. The group included those in public health, psychology, social work, spiritual life, publishing, business, accounting, and education. Some were experienced meditators; others were complete beginners. Thank you to Linda Wertheim, Nancy Henningsen, Lotte Lent, Allison Rains, Caroline Rains, Bill Rains, Ed Freedman, Harriet Freedman, Susan Freedman, Barbara Freedman, Deborah Benke, Kathleen Spiro, Gina Hass, Bruce Marshall, Suzie Kline Massey, and Lori Marks. Special thanks to my husband and daughters for their unyielding support, to my sister for providing valuable feedback throughout the entire project, and to my father for helping me develop the subtitle of the book.

ACKNOWLEDGMENTS

To the wordsmiths: Thank you to Barbara Kahl who brought exceptional depth, precision, and insight to this project with her substantive editing. Thank you to technical writer Sharon Meliker who brought her keen perspective and sharp eye. Thank you to copyeditor Wendy Paramore, who polished the final manuscript with astuteness and acuity. Thank you to editors Bob Hass and Karen Kullgren for their detailed reviews of the early stages of the manuscript.

To my book designer and my illustrator: Thank you to Anne Kachergis of Kachergis Book Design for her vision in transforming a typed manuscript into a beautiful primer. Thank you to illustrator Natalie Goldsmith for the wonderful, peaceful sitting meditation figures.

To my teachers, some of whom I know only through your written words: Thank you to Thich Nhat Hanh, Mata Amritanandamayi, Paramhansa Yogananda, Tilden Edwards, Eknath Easwaran, Hugh Byrne.

To the participants in my programs, who have been the source of much inspiration.

For all that each of you brings, I am deeply grateful.

Whole Earth Press is a small publishing group in Bethesda, MD. We are dedicated to offering publications that can help heal the whole person, whole communities, and the whole earth.

www.wholeearthpress.com

CPSIA information can be obtained
at www.ICGtesting.com
Printed in the USA
FFOW03n0007091214
9301FF